50 Pasta Dish Recipes for Home

By: Kelly Johnson

Table of Contents

- Spaghetti Carbonara
- Fettuccine Alfredo
- Penne Arrabbiata
- Linguine with Clam Sauce
- Lasagna Bolognese
- Rigatoni alla Vodka
- Pesto Pasta
- Pasta Primavera
- Macaroni and Cheese
- Shrimp Scampi Linguine
- Chicken Alfredo Pasta
- Mushroom Risotto
- Baked Ziti
- Tortellini with Pesto Cream Sauce
- Spinach and Ricotta Stuffed Shells
- Lemon Garlic Shrimp Pasta
- Spaghetti Aglio e Olio
- Gnocchi with Tomato Sauce
- Ravioli with Sage Butter Sauce
- Pasta e Fagioli
- Beef Stroganoff
- Caprese Pasta Salad
- Crab Linguine
- Chicken Piccata with Angel Hair Pasta
- Beef Ragu with Pappardelle
- Pasta Puttanesca
- Shrimp Linguine with White Wine Sauce
- Butternut Squash Ravioli
- Creamy Mushroom Pasta
- Seafood Paella
- Eggplant Parmesan
- Lobster Ravioli with Tomato Cream Sauce
- Pasta with Roasted Vegetables
- Creamy Chicken and Broccoli Pasta
- Lemon Asparagus Pasta

- Spaghetti with Meatballs
- Sun-Dried Tomato Pesto Pasta
- Cajun Shrimp Pasta
- Pasta with Sausage and Peppers
- Baked Manicotti
- Mediterranean Orzo Salad
- Tuna Casserole
- Pasta with Roasted Garlic and Cherry Tomatoes
- Pumpkin Ravioli with Brown Butter Sage Sauce
- Chicken and Spinach Alfredo Lasagna
- Penne alla Norma
- Pasta with Artichokes and Sun-Dried Tomatoes
- Beef and Mushroom Stroganoff
- Creamy Bacon Carbonara
- Spicy Arrabbiata Pasta

Spaghetti Carbonara

Ingredients:

- 350g spaghetti
- 150g pancetta or guanciale, diced
- 3 large eggs
- 100g grated Pecorino Romano cheese (or Parmesan)
- Freshly ground black pepper
- Salt (for pasta water)

Instructions:

1. Bring a large pot of salted water to a boil. Cook the spaghetti according to the package instructions until al dente.
2. While the pasta is cooking, heat a large skillet over medium heat. Add the diced pancetta or guanciale and cook until crispy and golden brown, about 5-7 minutes. Remove from heat and set aside.
3. In a mixing bowl, whisk together the eggs, grated cheese, and a generous amount of freshly ground black pepper.
4. Once the pasta is cooked, reserve about 1/2 cup of the pasta cooking water, then drain the spaghetti and return it to the pot.
5. Quickly pour the egg and cheese mixture over the hot spaghetti, tossing continuously to coat the pasta evenly. The heat from the pasta will cook the eggs and melt the cheese, creating a creamy sauce. If the sauce seems too thick, add a little of the reserved pasta water to loosen it up.
6. Add the cooked pancetta or guanciale to the pasta and toss to combine.
7. Serve immediately, garnished with extra grated cheese and black pepper if desired.

Enjoy your delicious Spaghetti Carbonara!

Fettuccine Alfredo

Ingredients:

- 8 ounces (about 225g) fettuccine pasta
- 1/2 cup (1 stick) unsalted butter
- 1 cup heavy cream
- 1 cup freshly grated Parmesan cheese
- Salt and freshly ground black pepper, to taste
- Optional: chopped parsley for garnish

Instructions:

1. Cook the fettuccine pasta according to the package instructions until it's al dente. Drain the pasta and set it aside, reserving about 1/2 cup of the pasta cooking water.
2. In a large skillet or saucepan, melt the butter over medium heat.
3. Once the butter has melted, add the heavy cream to the skillet. Stir continuously until the mixture starts to simmer.
4. Reduce the heat to low and gradually whisk in the grated Parmesan cheese, stirring constantly until the cheese has melted and the sauce is smooth and creamy. Be careful not to let the sauce boil.
5. Season the sauce with salt and freshly ground black pepper to taste. If the sauce seems too thick, you can thin it out by adding some of the reserved pasta cooking water, a little at a time, until you reach your desired consistency.
6. Add the cooked fettuccine pasta to the skillet with the sauce. Toss the pasta gently until it's evenly coated with the sauce.
7. Serve the Fettuccine Alfredo hot, garnished with chopped parsley if desired. You can also sprinkle some additional grated Parmesan cheese on top before serving.

Enjoy your delicious homemade Fettuccine Alfredo!

Penne Arrabbiata

Ingredients:

- 12 ounces (about 340g) penne pasta
- 2 tablespoons olive oil
- 4 cloves garlic, minced
- 1/2 teaspoon red pepper flakes (adjust to taste for desired level of spiciness)
- 1 (28-ounce) can crushed tomatoes
- 1 teaspoon sugar
- Salt, to taste
- Freshly ground black pepper, to taste
- Fresh basil leaves, torn, for garnish (optional)
- Grated Parmesan cheese, for serving (optional)

Instructions:

1. Cook the penne pasta according to the package instructions until al dente. Drain the pasta and set it aside.
2. In a large skillet, heat the olive oil over medium heat. Add the minced garlic and red pepper flakes to the skillet. Cook, stirring constantly, for about 1 minute or until the garlic is fragrant and just beginning to turn golden.
3. Pour the crushed tomatoes into the skillet, stirring to combine with the garlic and red pepper flakes. Bring the sauce to a simmer.
4. Add the sugar to the sauce, stirring to combine. The sugar helps balance the acidity of the tomatoes.
5. Season the sauce with salt and freshly ground black pepper to taste. Simmer the sauce for about 10-15 minutes, stirring occasionally, until it thickens slightly.
6. Once the sauce has thickened, add the cooked penne pasta to the skillet. Toss the pasta gently until it's evenly coated with the sauce.
7. Serve the Penne Arrabbiata hot, garnished with torn fresh basil leaves if desired. You can also sprinkle some grated Parmesan cheese on top before serving for added flavor.

Enjoy your spicy and flavorful Penne Arrabbiata!

Linguine with Clam Sauce

Ingredients:

- 12 ounces (about 340g) linguine pasta
- 2 tablespoons olive oil
- 4 cloves garlic, minced
- 1/4 teaspoon red pepper flakes (adjust to taste)
- 1/2 cup dry white wine
- 2 dozen littleneck clams, scrubbed and cleaned
- 1/4 cup chopped fresh parsley
- Salt, to taste
- Freshly ground black pepper, to taste
- Grated Parmesan cheese, for serving (optional)
- Lemon wedges, for serving (optional)

Instructions:

1. Cook the linguine pasta according to the package instructions until al dente. Drain the pasta and set it aside.
2. In a large skillet, heat the olive oil over medium heat. Add the minced garlic and red pepper flakes to the skillet. Cook, stirring constantly, for about 1 minute or until the garlic is fragrant.
3. Pour the white wine into the skillet, stirring to deglaze the pan. Bring the wine to a simmer.
4. Add the cleaned clams to the skillet. Cover the skillet with a lid and cook for about 5-7 minutes, or until the clams have opened. Discard any clams that do not open.
5. Once the clams have opened, remove them from the skillet and set them aside. Keep the skillet with the cooking liquid on the heat.
6. Add the cooked linguine pasta to the skillet with the cooking liquid. Toss the pasta gently until it's evenly coated with the liquid.
7. Remove the clams from their shells and chop them into bite-sized pieces. Add the chopped clams back to the skillet with the pasta.
8. Stir in the chopped fresh parsley, and season the pasta with salt and freshly ground black pepper to taste.
9. Serve the Linguine with Clam Sauce hot, garnished with grated Parmesan cheese and lemon wedges if desired.

Enjoy your delicious Linguine with Clam Sauce!

Lasagna Bolognese

Ingredients:

For the Bolognese sauce:

- 1 tablespoon olive oil
- 1 onion, finely chopped
- 2 carrots, finely chopped
- 2 celery stalks, finely chopped
- 4 cloves garlic, minced
- 1 pound (450g) ground beef
- 1/2 pound (225g) ground pork
- 1/2 cup (120ml) dry red wine
- 1 can (28 ounces/800g) crushed tomatoes
- 2 tablespoons tomato paste
- 1 teaspoon dried oregano
- 1 teaspoon dried basil
- Salt and freshly ground black pepper, to taste

For the béchamel sauce:

- 4 tablespoons unsalted butter
- 1/4 cup (30g) all-purpose flour
- 3 cups (720ml) whole milk
- Salt and freshly ground black pepper, to taste
- Pinch of nutmeg

For assembling:

- 12 lasagna noodles, cooked according to package instructions
- 2 cups (200g) shredded mozzarella cheese
- 1 cup (100g) grated Parmesan cheese

Instructions:

1. To make the Bolognese sauce, heat the olive oil in a large skillet over medium heat. Add the onion, carrots, and celery, and cook until softened, about 5 minutes. Add the garlic and cook for an additional minute.
2. Add the ground beef and pork to the skillet, breaking it up with a spoon, and cook until browned.

3. Stir in the red wine, crushed tomatoes, tomato paste, oregano, basil, salt, and pepper. Bring to a simmer and cook for about 30 minutes, stirring occasionally, until the sauce thickens.
4. Meanwhile, prepare the béchamel sauce. In a saucepan, melt the butter over medium heat. Stir in the flour and cook for 1-2 minutes, until golden brown. Gradually whisk in the milk, and cook, stirring constantly, until the sauce thickens. Season with salt, pepper, and nutmeg.
5. Preheat the oven to 375°F (190°C).
6. To assemble the lasagna, spread a thin layer of Bolognese sauce on the bottom of a 9x13-inch baking dish. Place a layer of cooked lasagna noodles on top. Spread a layer of Bolognese sauce over the noodles, followed by a layer of béchamel sauce and a sprinkle of mozzarella and Parmesan cheese. Repeat the layers, finishing with a layer of cheese on top.
7. Cover the baking dish with aluminum foil and bake in the preheated oven for 25 minutes. Remove the foil and bake for an additional 10-15 minutes, until the cheese is golden and bubbly.
8. Let the lasagna cool for a few minutes before slicing and serving.

Enjoy your homemade Lasagna Bolognese!

Rigatoni alla Vodka

Ingredients:

- 12 ounces (about 340g) rigatoni pasta
- 2 tablespoons olive oil
- 4 cloves garlic, minced
- 1/2 teaspoon red pepper flakes (adjust to taste)
- 1 cup vodka
- 1 can (28 ounces/800g) crushed tomatoes
- 1 cup heavy cream
- 1/2 cup grated Parmesan cheese
- Salt and freshly ground black pepper, to taste
- Fresh basil leaves, torn, for garnish (optional)

Instructions:

1. Cook the rigatoni pasta according to the package instructions until al dente. Drain the pasta and set it aside.
2. In a large skillet, heat the olive oil over medium heat. Add the minced garlic and red pepper flakes to the skillet. Cook, stirring constantly, for about 1 minute or until the garlic is fragrant.
3. Carefully pour the vodka into the skillet, stirring to deglaze the pan. Let the vodka simmer for a few minutes until it reduces slightly.
4. Add the crushed tomatoes to the skillet, stirring to combine with the vodka and garlic mixture. Bring the sauce to a simmer and let it cook for about 10-15 minutes, stirring occasionally, until it thickens slightly.
5. Stir in the heavy cream and grated Parmesan cheese until the sauce is smooth and creamy. Season with salt and freshly ground black pepper to taste.
6. Add the cooked rigatoni pasta to the skillet with the sauce. Toss the pasta gently until it's evenly coated with the sauce.
7. Serve the Rigatoni alla Vodka hot, garnished with torn fresh basil leaves if desired.

Enjoy your delicious Rigatoni alla Vodka!

Pesto Pasta

Ingredients:

- 12 ounces (about 340g) pasta (traditionally, long, thin pasta like spaghetti or fettuccine is used, but you can use any type you prefer)
- 2 cups fresh basil leaves, packed
- 2 cloves garlic, peeled
- 1/3 cup pine nuts (you can also use walnuts or almonds)
- 1/2 cup grated Parmesan cheese
- 1/2 cup extra virgin olive oil
- Salt and freshly ground black pepper, to taste
- Optional: additional grated Parmesan cheese and fresh basil leaves for garnish

Instructions:

1. Cook the pasta according to the package instructions until it reaches al dente texture. Drain it, reserving about 1/2 cup of the pasta cooking water, and return it to the pot.
2. While the pasta is cooking, prepare the pesto sauce. In a food processor or blender, combine the basil leaves, garlic, pine nuts, and grated Parmesan cheese.
3. Pulse the mixture until the ingredients are finely chopped.
4. With the food processor or blender running, gradually drizzle in the olive oil until the mixture is smooth and well combined. You may need to stop and scrape down the sides of the bowl with a spatula to ensure everything is evenly mixed.
5. Season the pesto sauce with salt and freshly ground black pepper to taste.
6. Pour the pesto sauce over the cooked pasta in the pot and toss until the pasta is evenly coated. If the sauce seems too thick, you can add some of the reserved pasta cooking water to thin it out.
7. Serve the pesto pasta hot, garnished with additional grated Parmesan cheese and fresh basil leaves if desired.

Enjoy your delightful pesto pasta! It's a simple yet incredibly flavorful dish that's perfect for any occasion.

Pasta Primavera

Ingredients:

- 12 ounces (about 340g) pasta (linguine, fettuccine, or penne work well)
- 2 tablespoons olive oil
- 2 cloves garlic, minced
- 1 small onion, thinly sliced
- 1 bell pepper, thinly sliced (any color you prefer)
- 1 small zucchini, thinly sliced
- 1 small yellow squash, thinly sliced
- 1 cup cherry tomatoes, halved
- 1 cup broccoli florets
- 1 cup snap peas or sugar snap peas, trimmed
- 1/2 cup grated Parmesan cheese
- Salt and freshly ground black pepper, to taste
- Optional: red pepper flakes for added heat
- Fresh basil leaves, torn, for garnish

Instructions:

1. Cook the pasta according to the package instructions until al dente. Drain and set aside, reserving about 1/2 cup of the pasta cooking water.
2. In a large skillet, heat the olive oil over medium heat. Add the minced garlic and sliced onion, and sauté until the onion is translucent and fragrant, about 2-3 minutes.
3. Add the sliced bell pepper, zucchini, yellow squash, cherry tomatoes, broccoli florets, and snap peas to the skillet. Season with salt and freshly ground black pepper to taste. Optionally, you can add red pepper flakes for extra heat.
4. Cook the vegetables until they are tender-crisp, stirring occasionally, about 5-7 minutes.
5. Add the cooked pasta to the skillet with the vegetables. Toss everything together, adding a splash of the reserved pasta cooking water if needed to loosen the pasta.
6. Sprinkle the grated Parmesan cheese over the pasta and vegetables, and toss again until the cheese is melted and everything is evenly coated.
7. Taste and adjust seasoning if necessary.
8. Serve the Pasta Primavera hot, garnished with torn fresh basil leaves.

Enjoy your colorful and delicious Pasta Primavera! Feel free to customize it with your favorite seasonal vegetables or herbs.

Macaroni and Cheese

Ingredients:

- 8 ounces (about 225g) elbow macaroni or any pasta shape you prefer
- 4 tablespoons unsalted butter
- 1/4 cup all-purpose flour
- 2 cups whole milk
- 2 cups shredded cheese (such as sharp cheddar, mozzarella, or a blend)
- Salt and freshly ground black pepper, to taste
- Optional toppings: breadcrumbs, crispy bacon bits, chopped herbs

Instructions:

1. Preheat your oven to 350°F (175°C). Grease a baking dish with butter or cooking spray.
2. Cook the macaroni according to the package instructions in a large pot of salted boiling water until al dente. Drain and set aside.
3. In the same pot, melt the butter over medium heat. Once melted, whisk in the flour to create a roux. Cook, stirring constantly, for about 1-2 minutes to remove the raw flour taste.
4. Gradually pour in the milk, whisking constantly to prevent lumps from forming. Cook the sauce, stirring frequently, until it thickens and coats the back of a spoon, about 5-7 minutes.
5. Reduce the heat to low and stir in the shredded cheese, reserving some for topping if desired. Continue stirring until the cheese is melted and the sauce is smooth. Season with salt and pepper to taste.
6. Add the cooked macaroni to the cheese sauce and stir until evenly coated.
7. Pour the macaroni and cheese mixture into the prepared baking dish. If desired, sprinkle additional shredded cheese on top for a crispy, cheesy crust.
8. Bake in the preheated oven for 20-25 minutes, or until the cheese is bubbly and golden brown on top.
9. Let the macaroni and cheese cool for a few minutes before serving. If desired, garnish with breadcrumbs, crispy bacon bits, or chopped herbs before serving.

Enjoy your homemade macaroni and cheese, a timeless comfort food favorite!

Shrimp Scampi Linguine

Ingredients:

- 12 ounces (about 340g) linguine pasta
- 1 pound (about 450g) large shrimp, peeled and deveined
- Salt and freshly ground black pepper, to taste
- 4 tablespoons unsalted butter
- 4 cloves garlic, minced
- 1/4 teaspoon red pepper flakes (adjust to taste)
- 1/4 cup dry white wine (optional)
- 1/4 cup fresh lemon juice (from about 2 lemons)
- Zest of 1 lemon
- 1/4 cup chopped fresh parsley
- Grated Parmesan cheese, for serving (optional)
- Lemon wedges, for serving (optional)

Instructions:

1. Cook the linguine pasta according to the package instructions until al dente. Drain the pasta and set it aside.
2. Season the shrimp with salt and pepper to taste.
3. In a large skillet, melt 2 tablespoons of butter over medium heat. Add the minced garlic and red pepper flakes to the skillet and sauté until fragrant, about 1 minute.
4. Add the seasoned shrimp to the skillet in a single layer. Cook for 2-3 minutes per side, or until the shrimp are pink and opaque. Be careful not to overcook them. Remove the cooked shrimp from the skillet and set them aside.
5. In the same skillet, add the remaining 2 tablespoons of butter. If using, pour in the white wine and lemon juice, and let the mixture simmer for 1-2 minutes, allowing the alcohol to cook off.
6. Add the cooked linguine pasta to the skillet, along with the lemon zest and chopped parsley. Toss everything together until the pasta is coated evenly with the sauce.
7. Return the cooked shrimp to the skillet and toss gently to combine with the pasta.
8. Serve the Shrimp Scampi Linguine hot, garnished with grated Parmesan cheese and lemon wedges if desired.

Enjoy your delicious Shrimp Scampi Linguine, a perfect blend of flavors and textures!

Chicken Alfredo Pasta

Ingredients:

- 8 ounces (about 225g) fettuccine pasta
- 2 boneless, skinless chicken breasts, thinly sliced
- Salt and freshly ground black pepper, to taste
- 2 tablespoons olive oil
- 4 tablespoons unsalted butter
- 4 cloves garlic, minced
- 1 cup heavy cream
- 1 cup grated Parmesan cheese, plus extra for serving
- 2 tablespoons chopped fresh parsley, for garnish (optional)

Instructions:

1. Cook the fettuccine pasta according to the package instructions until al dente. Drain the pasta and set it aside.
2. Season the chicken breast strips with salt and pepper to taste.
3. In a large skillet, heat the olive oil over medium-high heat. Add the seasoned chicken breast strips to the skillet and cook until they are golden brown and cooked through, about 4-5 minutes per side. Remove the cooked chicken from the skillet and set it aside.
4. In the same skillet, melt the butter over medium heat. Add the minced garlic to the skillet and sauté until fragrant, about 1 minute.
5. Pour the heavy cream into the skillet and bring it to a simmer, stirring constantly.
6. Gradually whisk in the grated Parmesan cheese, stirring until the cheese is melted and the sauce is smooth and creamy.
7. Add the cooked fettuccine pasta and cooked chicken breast strips to the skillet with the Alfredo sauce. Toss everything together until the pasta and chicken are evenly coated with the sauce.
8. Serve the Chicken Alfredo Pasta hot, garnished with chopped fresh parsley and extra grated Parmesan cheese if desired.

Enjoy your delicious and comforting Chicken Alfredo Pasta! It's perfect for a cozy dinner at home or for entertaining guests.

Mushroom Risotto

Ingredients:

- 1 cup Arborio rice
- 4 cups vegetable or chicken broth (keep warm)
- 2 tablespoons olive oil
- 2 tablespoons unsalted butter
- 1 onion, finely chopped
- 2 cloves garlic, minced
- 8 ounces (about 225g) mushrooms (such as cremini, shiitake, or button), sliced
- 1/2 cup dry white wine (optional)
- 1/2 cup grated Parmesan cheese
- Salt and freshly ground black pepper, to taste
- Chopped fresh parsley, for garnish (optional)

Instructions:

1. In a large saucepan or Dutch oven, heat the olive oil and butter over medium heat. Add the chopped onion and cook until it becomes translucent, about 3-4 minutes. Add the minced garlic and cook for an additional minute, stirring frequently.
2. Add the sliced mushrooms to the saucepan and cook until they are softened and golden brown, about 5-7 minutes.
3. Stir in the Arborio rice and cook for 1-2 minutes, stirring constantly, until the rice is well-coated with the oil and butter mixture.
4. If using, pour in the white wine and cook until it is absorbed by the rice, stirring occasionally.
5. Begin adding the warm broth to the rice mixture, one ladleful at a time, stirring frequently. Allow each addition of broth to be absorbed by the rice before adding more. Continue this process until the rice is cooked al dente and has a creamy texture, which should take about 20-25 minutes.
6. Once the rice is cooked to your desired consistency, stir in the grated Parmesan cheese until it is melted and well-incorporated into the risotto. Season with salt and freshly ground black pepper to taste.
7. Serve the mushroom risotto hot, garnished with chopped fresh parsley if desired.

Enjoy your creamy and flavorful Mushroom Risotto as a comforting main dish or as a side to accompany your favorite protein!

Baked Ziti

Ingredients:

- 1 pound (about 450g) ziti pasta
- 1 tablespoon olive oil
- 1 onion, chopped
- 2 cloves garlic, minced
- 1 pound (about 450g) ground beef or Italian sausage (optional)
- 1 jar (24-ounce) marinara sauce
- 1 cup ricotta cheese
- 1 cup shredded mozzarella cheese, divided
- 1/2 cup grated Parmesan cheese
- 2 tablespoons chopped fresh parsley
- Salt and freshly ground black pepper, to taste

Instructions:

1. Preheat your oven to 375°F (190°C). Grease a 9x13-inch baking dish with cooking spray or butter.
2. Cook the ziti pasta according to the package instructions until al dente. Drain the pasta and set it aside.
3. In a large skillet, heat the olive oil over medium heat. Add the chopped onion and minced garlic, and cook until softened and fragrant, about 3-4 minutes.
4. If using, add the ground beef or Italian sausage to the skillet. Cook, breaking it up with a spoon, until browned and cooked through. Drain any excess grease if necessary.
5. Pour the marinara sauce into the skillet with the cooked meat and onions. Stir to combine, and let the mixture simmer for about 5 minutes. Season with salt and pepper to taste.
6. In a large bowl, combine the cooked ziti pasta, ricotta cheese, half of the shredded mozzarella cheese, grated Parmesan cheese, chopped parsley, and half of the marinara sauce mixture. Mix until everything is well combined.
7. Pour the pasta mixture into the prepared baking dish. Spread the remaining marinara sauce over the top of the pasta.
8. Sprinkle the remaining shredded mozzarella cheese over the top of the pasta.
9. Cover the baking dish with aluminum foil and bake in the preheated oven for 25 minutes.
10. Remove the foil and bake for an additional 10-15 minutes, or until the cheese is melted and bubbly and the edges are golden brown.

11. Let the baked ziti cool for a few minutes before serving.

Enjoy your delicious and comforting Baked Ziti! It pairs well with a side salad and garlic bread for a complete meal.

Tortellini with Pesto Cream Sauce

Ingredients:

- 1 pound (about 450g) cheese-filled tortellini (fresh or frozen)
- 1/2 cup prepared pesto sauce (store-bought or homemade)
- 1 cup heavy cream
- 1/4 cup grated Parmesan cheese
- Salt and freshly ground black pepper, to taste
- Optional toppings: toasted pine nuts, chopped fresh basil, additional grated Parmesan cheese

Instructions:

1. Cook the tortellini according to the package instructions until al dente. Drain the tortellini and set it aside.
2. In a large skillet, heat the heavy cream over medium heat until it starts to simmer.
3. Stir in the prepared pesto sauce and grated Parmesan cheese until well combined. Continue to cook, stirring frequently, until the sauce thickens slightly, about 2-3 minutes. Season with salt and freshly ground black pepper to taste.
4. Add the cooked tortellini to the skillet with the pesto cream sauce. Toss gently until the tortellini is evenly coated with the sauce and heated through.
5. Serve the Tortellini with Pesto Cream Sauce hot, garnished with toasted pine nuts, chopped fresh basil, and additional grated Parmesan cheese if desired.

Enjoy your delicious and creamy Tortellini with Pesto Cream Sauce! It's a perfect dish for a quick and satisfying weeknight dinner.

Spinach and Ricotta Stuffed Shells

Ingredients:

- 1 box (12 ounces) jumbo pasta shells
- 1 tablespoon olive oil
- 1 small onion, finely chopped
- 2 cloves garlic, minced
- 1 (10-ounce) package frozen chopped spinach, thawed and drained
- 1 (15-ounce) container ricotta cheese
- 1 cup shredded mozzarella cheese, divided
- 1/2 cup grated Parmesan cheese
- 1 large egg
- 1 teaspoon dried oregano
- 1 teaspoon dried basil
- Salt and freshly ground black pepper, to taste
- 2 cups marinara sauce

Instructions:

1. Preheat your oven to 375°F (190°C). Grease a 9x13-inch baking dish with cooking spray or butter.
2. Cook the jumbo pasta shells according to the package instructions until al dente. Drain the shells and rinse them under cold water to stop the cooking process. Set aside.
3. In a skillet, heat the olive oil over medium heat. Add the chopped onion and minced garlic, and cook until softened and fragrant, about 3-4 minutes.
4. Add the thawed and drained spinach to the skillet. Cook for an additional 2-3 minutes, stirring occasionally, until any excess moisture from the spinach has evaporated. Remove from heat and let it cool slightly.
5. In a large mixing bowl, combine the cooked spinach mixture, ricotta cheese, 1/2 cup shredded mozzarella cheese, grated Parmesan cheese, egg, dried oregano, dried basil, salt, and black pepper. Mix until well combined.
6. Spread half of the marinara sauce evenly over the bottom of the prepared baking dish.
7. Stuff each cooked pasta shell with a spoonful of the spinach and ricotta mixture, and place them in the baking dish.
8. Once all the shells are stuffed and arranged in the baking dish, spoon the remaining marinara sauce over the top of the shells.

9. Sprinkle the remaining 1/2 cup shredded mozzarella cheese over the top of the sauce.
10. Cover the baking dish with aluminum foil and bake in the preheated oven for 25 minutes.
11. Remove the foil and bake for an additional 10-15 minutes, or until the cheese is melted and bubbly.
12. Let the stuffed shells cool for a few minutes before serving.

Enjoy your delicious Spinach and Ricotta Stuffed Shells! Serve them with a side salad and garlic bread for a complete meal.

Lemon Garlic Shrimp Pasta

Ingredients:

- 8 ounces (about 225g) linguine or spaghetti pasta
- 1 pound (about 450g) large shrimp, peeled and deveined
- Salt and freshly ground black pepper, to taste
- 3 tablespoons unsalted butter
- 4 cloves garlic, minced
- Zest of 1 lemon
- Juice of 1 lemon
- 1/4 teaspoon red pepper flakes (optional)
- 1/4 cup chopped fresh parsley, plus extra for garnish
- Grated Parmesan cheese, for serving (optional)
- Lemon wedges, for serving (optional)

Instructions:

1. Cook the pasta according to the package instructions until al dente. Drain the pasta and set it aside.
2. Season the shrimp with salt and freshly ground black pepper to taste.
3. In a large skillet, melt the butter over medium heat. Add the minced garlic to the skillet and sauté until fragrant, about 1 minute.
4. Add the seasoned shrimp to the skillet in a single layer. Cook for 2-3 minutes per side, or until the shrimp are pink and opaque. Be careful not to overcook them. Remove the cooked shrimp from the skillet and set them aside.
5. In the same skillet, add the lemon zest, lemon juice, and red pepper flakes (if using). Stir to combine and let it simmer for 1-2 minutes.
6. Add the cooked pasta and chopped fresh parsley to the skillet with the lemon garlic sauce. Toss everything together until the pasta is evenly coated with the sauce.
7. Return the cooked shrimp to the skillet and toss gently to combine with the pasta.
8. Serve the Lemon Garlic Shrimp Pasta hot, garnished with additional chopped fresh parsley and grated Parmesan cheese if desired. Serve with lemon wedges on the side for extra flavor.

Enjoy your delicious and refreshing Lemon Garlic Shrimp Pasta! It's perfect for a quick and satisfying weeknight dinner.

Spaghetti Aglio e Olio

Ingredients:

- 8 ounces (about 225g) spaghetti
- 1/4 cup extra virgin olive oil
- 4 cloves garlic, thinly sliced
- 1/2 teaspoon red pepper flakes (adjust to taste)
- Salt, to taste
- Freshly ground black pepper, to taste
- 1/4 cup chopped fresh parsley
- Grated Parmesan cheese, for serving (optional)
- Lemon wedges, for serving (optional)

Instructions:

1. Cook the spaghetti in a large pot of salted boiling water until al dente, according to the package instructions. Reserve about 1/2 cup of pasta cooking water, then drain the spaghetti and set it aside.
2. In a large skillet, heat the olive oil over medium heat. Add the thinly sliced garlic and red pepper flakes to the skillet. Cook, stirring frequently, until the garlic is golden brown and fragrant, but not burnt, about 2-3 minutes.
3. Add the cooked spaghetti to the skillet with the garlic and red pepper flakes. Toss everything together, adding a splash of the reserved pasta cooking water if needed to loosen the pasta and create a light sauce.
4. Season the spaghetti aglio e olio with salt and freshly ground black pepper to taste. Stir in the chopped fresh parsley, reserving a little for garnish.
5. Serve the spaghetti aglio e olio hot, garnished with additional chopped fresh parsley and grated Parmesan cheese if desired. Serve with lemon wedges on the side for squeezing over the pasta just before eating, if desired.

Enjoy your delicious and flavorful Spaghetti Aglio e Olio! It's a perfect dish for a quick and satisfying meal, and it's also great for entertaining guests.

Gnocchi with Tomato Sauce

Ingredients:

- 1 pound (about 450g) gnocchi (store-bought or homemade)
- 2 tablespoons olive oil
- 2 cloves garlic, minced
- 1 (14-ounce/400g) can crushed tomatoes
- 1 teaspoon dried oregano
- 1 teaspoon dried basil
- Salt and freshly ground black pepper, to taste
- Pinch of red pepper flakes (optional)
- Grated Parmesan cheese, for serving
- Fresh basil leaves, torn, for garnish (optional)

Instructions:

1. Cook the gnocchi according to the package instructions until they float to the surface, indicating that they're cooked. Drain the gnocchi and set them aside.
2. In a large skillet, heat the olive oil over medium heat. Add the minced garlic to the skillet and sauté until fragrant, about 1 minute.
3. Pour the crushed tomatoes into the skillet with the garlic. Stir in the dried oregano, dried basil, salt, black pepper, and red pepper flakes (if using). Bring the sauce to a simmer and let it cook for about 5-7 minutes, stirring occasionally, to allow the flavors to meld and the sauce to thicken slightly.
4. Add the cooked gnocchi to the skillet with the tomato sauce. Gently toss everything together until the gnocchi are evenly coated with the sauce.
5. Serve the Gnocchi with Tomato Sauce hot, garnished with grated Parmesan cheese and torn fresh basil leaves if desired.

Enjoy your delicious and comforting Gnocchi with Tomato Sauce! It's a perfect dish for a quick and satisfying meal, and you can customize it with your favorite herbs or additional toppings like chopped fresh parsley or crushed red pepper flakes.

Ravioli with Sage Butter Sauce

Ingredients:

- 1 pound (about 450g) ravioli (cheese, meat, or your favorite filling)
- 1/2 cup (1 stick) unsalted butter
- 8-10 fresh sage leaves
- Salt, to taste
- Freshly ground black pepper, to taste
- Grated Parmesan cheese, for serving (optional)

Instructions:

1. Cook the ravioli according to the package instructions until al dente. Drain the ravioli and set them aside, reserving about 1/4 cup of the pasta cooking water.
2. In a large skillet, melt the butter over medium heat. Add the fresh sage leaves to the skillet and cook until the butter begins to foam and the sage leaves become fragrant and crispy, about 2-3 minutes. Be careful not to burn the butter.
3. Once the butter is golden brown and aromatic, remove the skillet from the heat. Discard the sage leaves or leave them in the sauce for added flavor, depending on your preference.
4. Carefully add the cooked ravioli to the skillet with the sage-infused butter sauce. Toss gently to coat the ravioli evenly with the sauce. If the sauce is too thick, you can add a splash of the reserved pasta cooking water to thin it out.
5. Season the ravioli with salt and freshly ground black pepper to taste.
6. Serve the Ravioli with Sage Butter Sauce hot, garnished with grated Parmesan cheese if desired.

Enjoy your delicious and comforting Ravioli with Sage Butter Sauce! It's a perfect dish for a special occasion or a cozy dinner at home.

Pasta e Fagioli

Ingredients:

- 1 tablespoon olive oil
- 1 onion, chopped
- 2 cloves garlic, minced
- 2 carrots, diced
- 2 celery stalks, diced
- 1 can (15 ounces) cannellini beans, drained and rinsed
- 1 can (14.5 ounces) diced tomatoes
- 4 cups vegetable or chicken broth
- 1 teaspoon dried oregano
- 1 teaspoon dried basil
- 1/2 teaspoon dried thyme
- Salt and freshly ground black pepper, to taste
- 1 cup small pasta (such as ditalini, small shells, or elbow macaroni)
- Fresh parsley, chopped, for garnish (optional)
- Grated Parmesan cheese, for serving (optional)

Instructions:

1. In a large pot or Dutch oven, heat the olive oil over medium heat. Add the chopped onion, minced garlic, diced carrots, and diced celery. Cook, stirring occasionally, until the vegetables are softened, about 5-7 minutes.
2. Add the drained and rinsed cannellini beans, diced tomatoes (with their juices), vegetable or chicken broth, dried oregano, dried basil, and dried thyme to the pot. Season with salt and freshly ground black pepper to taste.
3. Bring the soup to a simmer, then reduce the heat to low and let it cook for about 15-20 minutes to allow the flavors to meld together.
4. In the meantime, cook the pasta separately according to the package instructions until al dente. Drain the pasta and set it aside.
5. Once the soup has simmered and the vegetables are tender, add the cooked pasta to the pot. Stir to combine, and let the soup simmer for an additional 5 minutes to heat through.
6. Taste and adjust seasoning if necessary.
7. Serve the Pasta e Fagioli hot, garnished with chopped fresh parsley and grated Parmesan cheese if desired. Enjoy!

Feel free to customize this recipe by adding other vegetables, such as diced zucchini or spinach, or by using different types of beans or pasta shapes.

Beef Stroganoff

Ingredients:

- 1 pound (about 450g) beef sirloin or tenderloin, thinly sliced
- Salt and freshly ground black pepper, to taste
- 2 tablespoons olive oil
- 1 onion, thinly sliced
- 2 cloves garlic, minced
- 8 ounces (about 225g) mushrooms, sliced
- 1 tablespoon all-purpose flour
- 1 cup beef broth
- 1 tablespoon Worcestershire sauce
- 1 cup sour cream
- 1 tablespoon Dijon mustard
- 1 tablespoon chopped fresh parsley, for garnish (optional)
- Cooked egg noodles or rice, for serving

Instructions:

1. Season the thinly sliced beef with salt and freshly ground black pepper to taste.
2. Heat the olive oil in a large skillet over medium-high heat. Add the seasoned beef slices to the skillet and cook until browned on all sides, about 3-4 minutes. Remove the beef from the skillet and set it aside.
3. In the same skillet, add the sliced onion and cook until softened, about 3-4 minutes. Add the minced garlic and sliced mushrooms to the skillet and cook for an additional 4-5 minutes, until the mushrooms are browned and any liquid has evaporated.
4. Sprinkle the flour over the mushrooms and onions in the skillet. Stir well to combine and cook for 1-2 minutes to remove the raw flour taste.
5. Gradually pour in the beef broth and Worcestershire sauce, stirring constantly to prevent lumps from forming. Bring the mixture to a simmer and cook until the sauce thickens slightly, about 3-4 minutes.
6. Return the cooked beef slices to the skillet and stir to coat them evenly with the sauce. Cook for an additional 2-3 minutes to heat through.
7. In a small bowl, mix together the sour cream and Dijon mustard until smooth. Stir the sour cream mixture into the skillet with the beef and sauce, and cook for 1-2 minutes until heated through.
8. Taste and adjust seasoning if necessary.

9. Serve the Beef Stroganoff hot, garnished with chopped fresh parsley if desired, and accompanied by cooked egg noodles or rice.

Enjoy your delicious Beef Stroganoff! It's a comforting and satisfying dish that's perfect for a cozy dinner at home.

Caprese Pasta Salad

Ingredients:

- 8 ounces (about 225g) pasta (such as penne, fusilli, or rotini)
- 2 cups cherry tomatoes, halved
- 8 ounces (about 225g) fresh mozzarella cheese, diced
- 1/4 cup fresh basil leaves, chopped
- 2 tablespoons extra virgin olive oil
- 2 tablespoons balsamic vinegar
- 1 clove garlic, minced
- Salt and freshly ground black pepper, to taste
- Optional: balsamic glaze for drizzling

Instructions:

1. Cook the pasta according to the package instructions until al dente. Drain the pasta and rinse it under cold water to stop the cooking process. Allow it to cool completely.
2. In a large bowl, combine the cooked and cooled pasta, halved cherry tomatoes, diced fresh mozzarella cheese, and chopped fresh basil leaves.
3. In a small bowl, whisk together the extra virgin olive oil, balsamic vinegar, minced garlic, salt, and freshly ground black pepper to make the dressing.
4. Pour the dressing over the pasta salad and toss gently to coat everything evenly.
5. Taste and adjust seasoning if necessary.
6. Optional: Drizzle the pasta salad with balsamic glaze for extra flavor and presentation.
7. Chill the Caprese Pasta Salad in the refrigerator for at least 30 minutes before serving to allow the flavors to meld together.
8. Serve the pasta salad cold as a refreshing side dish or light lunch.

Enjoy your delicious and vibrant Caprese Pasta Salad! It's perfect for picnics, potlucks, or as a refreshing summer meal.

Crab Linguine

Ingredients:

- 8 ounces (about 225g) linguine pasta
- 1 tablespoon olive oil
- 2 cloves garlic, minced
- 1/4 cup dry white wine
- 1 cup heavy cream
- 8 ounces (about 225g) lump crab meat, picked over for shells
- Zest and juice of 1 lemon
- Salt and freshly ground black pepper, to taste
- 2 tablespoons chopped fresh parsley, for garnish
- Grated Parmesan cheese, for serving (optional)

Instructions:

1. Cook the linguine pasta according to the package instructions until al dente. Drain the pasta and set it aside.
2. In a large skillet, heat the olive oil over medium heat. Add the minced garlic to the skillet and sauté until fragrant, about 1 minute.
3. Pour the white wine into the skillet and let it simmer for 1-2 minutes to reduce slightly.
4. Reduce the heat to medium-low and pour in the heavy cream. Stir to combine with the wine and garlic, and let the mixture simmer for about 3-4 minutes, until it begins to thicken slightly.
5. Add the lump crab meat to the skillet along with the lemon zest and lemon juice. Gently stir to combine and heat the crab through, being careful not to break up the crab meat too much. Season with salt and freshly ground black pepper to taste.
6. Add the cooked linguine pasta to the skillet with the crab and sauce. Toss everything together until the pasta is evenly coated with the sauce.
7. Serve the Crab Linguine hot, garnished with chopped fresh parsley and grated Parmesan cheese if desired.

Enjoy your delicious and indulgent Crab Linguine! It's perfect for a special occasion or a luxurious weeknight dinner.

Chicken Piccata with Angel Hair Pasta

Ingredients:

For the Chicken:

- 2 boneless, skinless chicken breasts, pounded to 1/4-inch thickness
- Salt and freshly ground black pepper, to taste
- 1/2 cup all-purpose flour, for dredging
- 2 tablespoons olive oil
- 2 tablespoons unsalted butter
- 1/2 cup dry white wine
- 1/2 cup chicken broth
- Juice of 1 lemon
- 2 tablespoons capers, drained
- 2 tablespoons chopped fresh parsley, for garnish

For the Angel Hair Pasta:

- 8 ounces (about 225g) angel hair pasta
- Salt, for cooking pasta
- 1 tablespoon olive oil
- 2 cloves garlic, minced
- 1 tablespoon chopped fresh parsley, for garnish

Instructions:

1. Season the pounded chicken breasts with salt and freshly ground black pepper on both sides. Dredge the chicken breasts in flour, shaking off any excess.
2. In a large skillet, heat the olive oil and butter over medium-high heat. Add the chicken breasts to the skillet and cook for 3-4 minutes on each side, or until golden brown and cooked through. Remove the chicken from the skillet and set it aside on a plate, covering loosely with foil to keep warm.
3. Deglaze the skillet with the white wine, scraping up any browned bits from the bottom of the pan. Let the wine cook for 1-2 minutes to reduce slightly.
4. Add the chicken broth, lemon juice, and capers to the skillet. Bring the sauce to a simmer and let it cook for about 5 minutes, or until slightly thickened. Taste and adjust seasoning if necessary.
5. While the sauce is simmering, cook the angel hair pasta according to the package instructions until al dente. Drain the pasta and set it aside.

6. In a separate skillet, heat the olive oil over medium heat. Add the minced garlic and cook until fragrant, about 1 minute.
7. Add the cooked angel hair pasta to the skillet with the garlic and toss to coat evenly with the oil. Season with salt to taste.
8. To serve, place a portion of angel hair pasta on each plate. Top with a cooked chicken breast and spoon the piccata sauce over the chicken. Garnish with chopped fresh parsley.
9. Serve the Chicken Piccata with Angel Hair Pasta hot, accompanied by your favorite side dishes or a crisp green salad.

Enjoy your delicious and flavorful Chicken Piccata with Angel Hair Pasta! It's a perfect dish for a special dinner or any day you want to treat yourself to a taste of Italy.

Beef Ragu with Pappardelle

Ingredients:

For the Beef Ragu:

- 2 pounds (about 900g) beef chuck roast, trimmed of excess fat and cut into chunks
- Salt and freshly ground black pepper, to taste
- 2 tablespoons olive oil
- 1 onion, finely chopped
- 2 carrots, finely chopped
- 2 celery stalks, finely chopped
- 4 cloves garlic, minced
- 1 tablespoon tomato paste
- 1 can (28 ounces/800g) crushed tomatoes
- 1 cup beef broth
- 1 cup red wine (such as Chianti or Cabernet Sauvignon)
- 2 bay leaves
- 1 teaspoon dried thyme
- 1 teaspoon dried oregano
- 1 teaspoon dried rosemary
- 1/4 teaspoon red pepper flakes (optional)
- Chopped fresh parsley, for garnish
- Grated Parmesan cheese, for serving (optional)

For the Pappardelle:

- 12 ounces (about 340g) pappardelle pasta
- Salt, for cooking pasta

Instructions:

1. Season the beef chunks with salt and freshly ground black pepper to taste.
2. In a large Dutch oven or heavy-bottomed pot, heat the olive oil over medium-high heat. Add the seasoned beef chunks to the pot in a single layer (you may need to do this in batches to avoid overcrowding the pot) and cook until browned on all sides, about 5-6 minutes per batch. Remove the browned beef from the pot and set it aside.

3. In the same pot, add the chopped onion, carrots, and celery. Cook, stirring occasionally, until the vegetables are softened, about 5 minutes. Add the minced garlic and cook for an additional 1-2 minutes until fragrant.
4. Stir in the tomato paste and cook for 1-2 minutes to caramelize it slightly.
5. Return the browned beef chunks to the pot. Add the crushed tomatoes, beef broth, red wine, bay leaves, dried thyme, dried oregano, dried rosemary, and red pepper flakes (if using). Stir to combine.
6. Bring the mixture to a simmer, then reduce the heat to low. Cover the pot and let the beef ragu simmer gently for 2-3 hours, stirring occasionally, until the beef is tender and the sauce has thickened. If the sauce becomes too thick during cooking, you can add a little more beef broth or water as needed.
7. While the beef ragu is simmering, cook the pappardelle pasta according to the package instructions until al dente. Drain the pasta and set it aside.
8. Once the beef is tender and the sauce has thickened to your liking, taste and adjust seasoning with salt and pepper if necessary. Remove the bay leaves.
9. To serve, spoon the beef ragu over the cooked pappardelle pasta. Garnish with chopped fresh parsley and grated Parmesan cheese if desired.

Enjoy your delicious and hearty Beef Ragu with Pappardelle! It's a comforting and satisfying meal that's perfect for special occasions or cozy family dinners.

Pasta Puttanesca

Ingredients:

- 12 ounces (about 340g) spaghetti or your favorite pasta shape
- 2 tablespoons olive oil
- 4 cloves garlic, minced
- 4 anchovy fillets, chopped (optional, but traditional)
- 1/4 teaspoon red pepper flakes (adjust to taste)
- 1 can (14.5 ounces/400g) diced tomatoes
- 1/4 cup sliced Kalamata olives
- 2 tablespoons capers, drained
- 2 tablespoons chopped fresh parsley, plus more for garnish
- Salt and freshly ground black pepper, to taste
- Grated Parmesan cheese, for serving (optional)

Instructions:

1. Cook the pasta according to the package instructions until al dente. Drain the pasta, reserving 1/2 cup of the pasta cooking water, and set aside.
2. In a large skillet, heat the olive oil over medium heat. Add the minced garlic, chopped anchovy fillets (if using), and red pepper flakes to the skillet. Cook, stirring frequently, for 1-2 minutes, or until the garlic is fragrant and the anchovies have melted into the oil.
3. Add the diced tomatoes (with their juices), sliced Kalamata olives, and drained capers to the skillet. Stir to combine.
4. Let the sauce simmer for 10-15 minutes, stirring occasionally, until it thickens slightly and the flavors meld together. If the sauce becomes too thick, you can add a splash of the reserved pasta cooking water to loosen it up.
5. Season the sauce with salt and freshly ground black pepper to taste. Stir in the chopped fresh parsley.
6. Add the cooked pasta to the skillet with the puttanesca sauce. Toss everything together until the pasta is evenly coated with the sauce.
7. Serve the Pasta Puttanesca hot, garnished with additional chopped fresh parsley and grated Parmesan cheese if desired.

Enjoy your delicious and flavorful Pasta Puttanesca! It's a quick and easy dish that's perfect for a weeknight dinner or anytime you're craving a taste of Italy.

Shrimp Linguine with White Wine Sauce

Ingredients:

- 8 ounces (about 225g) linguine pasta
- 1 pound (about 450g) large shrimp, peeled and deveined
- Salt and freshly ground black pepper, to taste
- 2 tablespoons unsalted butter
- 2 tablespoons olive oil
- 4 cloves garlic, minced
- 1/2 cup dry white wine (such as Pinot Grigio or Sauvignon Blanc)
- 1 cup heavy cream
- Zest and juice of 1 lemon
- 1/4 teaspoon red pepper flakes (optional)
- 2 tablespoons chopped fresh parsley, for garnish
- Grated Parmesan cheese, for serving (optional)

Instructions:

1. Cook the linguine pasta according to the package instructions until al dente. Drain the pasta and set it aside.
2. Season the shrimp with salt and freshly ground black pepper to taste.
3. In a large skillet, heat 1 tablespoon of butter and 1 tablespoon of olive oil over medium-high heat. Add the seasoned shrimp to the skillet and cook for 2-3 minutes per side, or until pink and opaque. Remove the cooked shrimp from the skillet and set them aside.
4. In the same skillet, add the remaining tablespoon of butter and olive oil. Add the minced garlic to the skillet and cook for 1-2 minutes, or until fragrant.
5. Pour the white wine into the skillet and let it simmer for 2-3 minutes to reduce slightly.
6. Stir in the heavy cream, lemon zest, lemon juice, and red pepper flakes (if using). Bring the sauce to a simmer and let it cook for 3-4 minutes, or until it thickens slightly.
7. Return the cooked shrimp to the skillet and toss to coat them evenly with the sauce. Cook for an additional 1-2 minutes to heat the shrimp through.
8. Add the cooked linguine pasta to the skillet with the shrimp and sauce. Toss everything together until the pasta is evenly coated with the sauce.
9. Serve the Shrimp Linguine with White Wine Sauce hot, garnished with chopped fresh parsley and grated Parmesan cheese if desired.

Enjoy your delicious and elegant Shrimp Linguine with White Wine Sauce! It's perfect for a special dinner or any time you want to impress your guests with a restaurant-quality dish.

Butternut Squash Ravioli

Ingredients:

For the Butternut Squash Filling:

- 1 small butternut squash (about 2 pounds/900g)
- 2 tablespoons olive oil
- Salt and freshly ground black pepper, to taste
- 1/4 teaspoon ground nutmeg
- 1/4 cup grated Parmesan cheese

For the Ravioli Dough:

- 2 cups all-purpose flour
- 3 large eggs
- 1/2 teaspoon salt

For the Sage Butter Sauce:

- 1/2 cup unsalted butter
- 8-10 fresh sage leaves
- Salt and freshly ground black pepper, to taste
- Grated Parmesan cheese, for serving (optional)

Instructions:

1. Preheat your oven to 400°F (200°C).
2. Cut the butternut squash in half lengthwise and scoop out the seeds. Brush the cut sides of the squash halves with olive oil and season with salt, freshly ground black pepper, and ground nutmeg.
3. Place the squash halves, cut side down, on a baking sheet lined with parchment paper. Roast in the preheated oven for 40-45 minutes, or until the squash is tender when pierced with a fork. Remove from the oven and let it cool slightly.
4. Scoop the roasted squash flesh into a bowl and mash it with a fork or potato masher until smooth. Stir in the grated Parmesan cheese and adjust seasoning with salt and pepper if necessary. Set aside to cool completely.
5. While the squash filling is cooling, make the ravioli dough. On a clean work surface, mound the flour and make a well in the center. Crack the eggs into the well and add the salt. Using a fork, gradually incorporate the flour into the eggs until a dough forms.

6. Knead the dough for 8-10 minutes, or until smooth and elastic. Wrap the dough in plastic wrap and let it rest at room temperature for at least 30 minutes.
7. Once the dough has rested, divide it into smaller portions and roll each portion out into thin sheets using a pasta machine or rolling pin.
8. Place small spoonfuls of the cooled butternut squash filling onto one sheet of pasta dough, leaving space between each mound of filling.
9. Brush the edges of the pasta dough with water and place another sheet of pasta dough on top, pressing down around each mound of filling to seal the ravioli.
10. Use a knife or ravioli cutter to cut out individual ravioli. Press down firmly around the edges to ensure they are well sealed.
11. Bring a large pot of salted water to a boil. Carefully add the ravioli to the boiling water and cook for 3-4 minutes, or until they float to the surface and are cooked through.
12. While the ravioli are cooking, make the sage butter sauce. In a skillet, melt the unsalted butter over medium heat. Add the fresh sage leaves and cook until the butter is golden brown and the sage leaves are crispy, about 3-4 minutes. Remove from heat.
13. Once the ravioli are cooked, use a slotted spoon to transfer them to the skillet with the sage butter sauce. Toss gently to coat the ravioli with the sauce.
14. Serve the Butternut Squash Ravioli hot, garnished with grated Parmesan cheese if desired.

Enjoy your delicious and homemade Butternut Squash Ravioli! It's a perfect dish for a special occasion or anytime you want to impress your guests with a gourmet meal.

Creamy Mushroom Pasta

Ingredients:

- 8 ounces (about 225g) pasta (such as fettuccine, linguine, or spaghetti)
- 2 tablespoons unsalted butter
- 2 tablespoons olive oil
- 1 pound (about 450g) mushrooms (such as cremini or button), sliced
- 4 cloves garlic, minced
- 1 cup heavy cream
- 1/2 cup chicken or vegetable broth
- 1/4 cup grated Parmesan cheese
- 2 tablespoons chopped fresh parsley
- Salt and freshly ground black pepper, to taste
- Optional: red pepper flakes, for heat

Instructions:

1. Cook the pasta according to the package instructions until al dente. Drain the pasta and set it aside, reserving 1/2 cup of the pasta cooking water.
2. In a large skillet, melt the butter with the olive oil over medium heat. Add the sliced mushrooms to the skillet and cook, stirring occasionally, until they are golden brown and tender, about 5-7 minutes.
3. Add the minced garlic to the skillet with the mushrooms and cook for an additional 1-2 minutes, or until fragrant.
4. Pour in the heavy cream and chicken or vegetable broth. Bring the mixture to a simmer and let it cook for 5-7 minutes, or until the sauce thickens slightly.
5. Stir in the grated Parmesan cheese and chopped fresh parsley. Season the sauce with salt and freshly ground black pepper to taste. If you like a bit of heat, you can also add red pepper flakes to taste.
6. Add the cooked pasta to the skillet with the creamy mushroom sauce. Toss everything together until the pasta is evenly coated with the sauce. If the sauce is too thick, you can add a splash of the reserved pasta cooking water to thin it out.
7. Serve the Creamy Mushroom Pasta hot, garnished with additional chopped fresh parsley and grated Parmesan cheese if desired.

Enjoy your delicious and comforting Creamy Mushroom Pasta! It's perfect for a cozy dinner at home or a special occasion meal.

Seafood Paella

Ingredients:

- 1 pound (about 450g) mixed seafood (such as shrimp, mussels, clams, squid, and/or firm white fish)
- 1 1/2 cups Spanish short-grain rice (such as Bomba or Calasparra rice)
- 3 cups chicken or seafood broth
- 1 onion, finely chopped
- 4 cloves garlic, minced
- 1 red bell pepper, diced
- 1 tomato, diced
- 1/2 cup frozen peas
- 1/2 teaspoon saffron threads
- 1 teaspoon smoked paprika
- Salt and freshly ground black pepper, to taste
- 2 tablespoons olive oil
- Lemon wedges, for serving
- Chopped fresh parsley, for garnish

Instructions:

1. If using shrimp, peel and devein them, leaving the tails intact. Clean the mussels and clams, discarding any that are open or broken. Rinse the squid and slice it into rings. Cut the firm white fish into bite-sized pieces. Set aside.
2. In a small bowl, crush the saffron threads with a mortar and pestle or the back of a spoon. Steep the crushed saffron threads in 1/4 cup of warm water for about 10-15 minutes to release the flavor and color.
3. In a large paella pan or skillet, heat the olive oil over medium heat. Add the chopped onion and diced red bell pepper to the pan and cook until softened, about 5 minutes. Add the minced garlic and cook for an additional 1-2 minutes, until fragrant.
4. Stir in the diced tomato and smoked paprika, and cook for another 2-3 minutes.
5. Add the rice to the pan and stir to coat it with the vegetable mixture. Cook for 1-2 minutes, stirring frequently, until the rice is lightly toasted.
6. Pour the saffron-infused water (including the saffron threads) into the pan, along with the chicken or seafood broth. Stir to combine.
7. Season the mixture with salt and freshly ground black pepper to taste. Bring the liquid to a simmer, then reduce the heat to low. Cover the pan with a lid or aluminum foil and let the rice cook for about 15 minutes, or until it's almost done.

8. Arrange the seafood on top of the partially cooked rice. Nestle the shrimp, mussels, clams, squid, and/or fish into the rice mixture, pressing them down slightly. Scatter the frozen peas evenly over the top.
9. Cover the pan again and continue cooking for another 10-15 minutes, or until the seafood is cooked through and the rice is tender. Make sure the mussels and clams have opened before serving.
10. Once the seafood paella is cooked, remove it from the heat and let it rest, covered, for a few minutes before serving.
11. Garnish the seafood paella with chopped fresh parsley and serve hot with lemon wedges on the side.

Enjoy your delicious and flavorful Seafood Paella! It's perfect for a festive gathering or a special dinner with family and friends.

Eggplant Parmesan

Ingredients:

- 2 large eggplants, sliced into 1/4-inch rounds
- Salt, for sweating the eggplant
- 1 cup all-purpose flour
- 3 large eggs, beaten
- 2 cups breadcrumbs (plain or Italian-seasoned)
- 1 cup grated Parmesan cheese
- 2 cups marinara sauce
- 2 cups shredded mozzarella cheese
- 1/4 cup chopped fresh basil, for garnish (optional)
- Olive oil, for frying

Instructions:

1. Preheat your oven to 375°F (190°C).
2. Place the eggplant slices in a colander and sprinkle them liberally with salt. Let them sit for about 30 minutes to draw out excess moisture. Rinse the eggplant slices under cold water and pat them dry with paper towels.
3. Set up a breading station with three shallow bowls: one with the flour, one with the beaten eggs, and one with the breadcrumbs mixed with grated Parmesan cheese.
4. Dredge each eggplant slice in the flour, shaking off any excess. Dip it into the beaten eggs, allowing any excess to drip off, then coat it thoroughly with the breadcrumb mixture. Repeat with the remaining eggplant slices.
5. Heat a thin layer of olive oil in a large skillet over medium-high heat. Working in batches, fry the breaded eggplant slices until golden brown and crispy, about 2-3 minutes per side. Transfer the fried eggplant slices to a paper towel-lined plate to drain excess oil.
6. Spread a thin layer of marinara sauce on the bottom of a baking dish. Arrange a layer of fried eggplant slices on top of the sauce, overlapping them slightly. Spoon more marinara sauce over the eggplant slices, then sprinkle with shredded mozzarella cheese.
7. Repeat the layers until all the eggplant slices are used, ending with a layer of marinara sauce and shredded mozzarella cheese on top.
8. Cover the baking dish with aluminum foil and bake in the preheated oven for 25-30 minutes, or until the cheese is melted and bubbly.

9. Remove the foil and continue baking for an additional 5-10 minutes, or until the cheese is golden brown and bubbly.
10. Remove the Eggplant Parmesan from the oven and let it cool for a few minutes before serving. Garnish with chopped fresh basil, if desired.
11. Serve the Eggplant Parmesan hot, accompanied by crusty bread or a side of pasta.

Enjoy your delicious and comforting Eggplant Parmesan! It's a perfect dish for a hearty vegetarian meal or as a side dish for a crowd-pleasing Italian feast.

Lobster Ravioli with Tomato Cream Sauce

Ingredients:

For the Lobster Ravioli:

- 1 pound (about 450g) fresh or frozen lobster meat, cooked and chopped
- 1/2 cup ricotta cheese
- 1/4 cup grated Parmesan cheese
- 2 tablespoons chopped fresh parsley
- 1 egg
- Salt and freshly ground black pepper, to taste
- 1 package (about 24 ounces/680g) fresh or frozen ravioli

For the Tomato Cream Sauce:

- 2 tablespoons olive oil
- 4 cloves garlic, minced
- 1/4 teaspoon red pepper flakes (adjust to taste)
- 1 can (14.5 ounces/400g) diced tomatoes
- 1 cup heavy cream
- Salt and freshly ground black pepper, to taste
- Chopped fresh basil, for garnish
- Grated Parmesan cheese, for serving (optional)

Instructions:

1. In a large mixing bowl, combine the cooked and chopped lobster meat, ricotta cheese, grated Parmesan cheese, chopped fresh parsley, and egg. Season with salt and freshly ground black pepper to taste. Mix well to combine.
2. Lay out the ravioli wrappers on a clean work surface. Place a small spoonful of the lobster mixture onto each wrapper. Brush the edges of the wrappers with water, then place another wrapper on top of each filled one. Press down firmly around the edges to seal the ravioli, ensuring there are no air pockets.
3. Bring a large pot of salted water to a boil. Carefully add the lobster ravioli to the boiling water and cook according to the package instructions, usually 3-4 minutes for fresh ravioli or 5-6 minutes for frozen ravioli. Drain the cooked ravioli and set them aside.
4. While the ravioli are cooking, prepare the tomato cream sauce. In a large skillet, heat the olive oil over medium heat. Add the minced garlic and red pepper flakes to the skillet and cook for 1-2 minutes, or until fragrant.

5. Stir in the diced tomatoes (with their juices) and cook for 5-7 minutes, or until the tomatoes start to break down and the sauce thickens slightly.
6. Pour in the heavy cream and stir to combine. Let the sauce simmer for another 5 minutes, or until it thickens to your desired consistency. Season with salt and freshly ground black pepper to taste.
7. Add the cooked lobster ravioli to the skillet with the tomato cream sauce. Gently toss to coat the ravioli evenly with the sauce.
8. Serve the Lobster Ravioli with Tomato Cream Sauce hot, garnished with chopped fresh basil and grated Parmesan cheese if desired.

Enjoy your delicious and indulgent Lobster Ravioli with Tomato Cream Sauce! It's perfect for a special occasion or any time you want to treat yourself to a gourmet meal.

Pasta with Roasted Vegetables

Ingredients:

- 1 pound (about 450g) pasta (such as penne, fusilli, or farfalle)
- Assorted vegetables, such as:
    - 2 bell peppers (red, yellow, or green), sliced
    - 1 zucchini, sliced
    - 1 yellow squash, sliced
    - 1 red onion, sliced
    - 1 cup cherry tomatoes, halved
    - 1 eggplant, diced
    - Any other vegetables of your choice (e.g., broccoli, cauliflower, carrots)
- 4 cloves garlic, minced
- 1/4 cup olive oil
- Salt and freshly ground black pepper, to taste
- Grated Parmesan cheese, for serving (optional)
- Chopped fresh basil or parsley, for garnish (optional)

Instructions:

1. Preheat your oven to 400°F (200°C).
2. In a large mixing bowl, toss the assorted vegetables with minced garlic and olive oil until evenly coated. Season with salt and freshly ground black pepper to taste.
3. Spread the vegetables in a single layer on a baking sheet lined with parchment paper or aluminum foil.
4. Roast the vegetables in the preheated oven for 20-25 minutes, or until they are tender and lightly browned, stirring occasionally to ensure even cooking.
5. While the vegetables are roasting, cook the pasta in a large pot of salted boiling water according to the package instructions until al dente. Drain the cooked pasta and set it aside.
6. Once the vegetables are roasted, remove them from the oven and toss them with the cooked pasta in a large mixing bowl.
7. Serve the pasta with roasted vegetables hot, garnished with grated Parmesan cheese and chopped fresh basil or parsley, if desired.
8. Enjoy your delicious and nutritious Pasta with Roasted Vegetables as a satisfying vegetarian meal or as a side dish for grilled meats or seafood.

Feel free to customize this recipe by adding your favorite vegetables or herbs. You can also drizzle some balsamic glaze or sprinkle some crushed red pepper flakes for added flavor.

Creamy Chicken and Broccoli Pasta

Ingredients:

- 8 ounces (about 225g) pasta (such as penne, fettuccine, or rotini)
- 2 boneless, skinless chicken breasts, cut into bite-sized pieces
- Salt and freshly ground black pepper, to taste
- 2 tablespoons olive oil
- 2 cloves garlic, minced
- 2 cups broccoli florets
- 1 cup chicken broth
- 1 cup heavy cream
- 1/2 cup grated Parmesan cheese
- 1 teaspoon Italian seasoning (or dried herbs of your choice)
- Red pepper flakes, to taste (optional)
- Chopped fresh parsley, for garnish

Instructions:

1. Cook the pasta according to the package instructions until al dente. Drain the pasta and set it aside.
2. Season the chicken pieces with salt and freshly ground black pepper to taste.
3. In a large skillet, heat the olive oil over medium-high heat. Add the seasoned chicken pieces to the skillet and cook until golden brown and cooked through, about 5-6 minutes per side. Remove the cooked chicken from the skillet and set it aside.
4. In the same skillet, add the minced garlic and cook for 1-2 minutes, or until fragrant.
5. Add the broccoli florets to the skillet and sauté for 3-4 minutes, or until they are tender-crisp.
6. Pour the chicken broth into the skillet and bring it to a simmer. Let it cook for 2-3 minutes, then stir in the heavy cream.
7. Stir in the grated Parmesan cheese and Italian seasoning. Add red pepper flakes, if using, for a bit of heat.
8. Return the cooked chicken to the skillet and toss everything together until the chicken and broccoli are coated with the creamy sauce.
9. Add the cooked pasta to the skillet and toss to combine, ensuring that the pasta is evenly coated with the sauce.
10. Cook for an additional 2-3 minutes, or until the pasta is heated through and the sauce has thickened slightly.

11. Serve the Creamy Chicken and Broccoli Pasta hot, garnished with chopped fresh parsley.

Enjoy your delicious and creamy Chicken and Broccoli Pasta! It's perfect for a cozy weeknight dinner or anytime you're craving a comforting meal.

Lemon Asparagus Pasta

Ingredients:

- 8 ounces (about 225g) pasta (such as linguine or spaghetti)
- 1 bunch asparagus, tough ends trimmed and cut into bite-sized pieces
- 2 tablespoons olive oil
- 3 cloves garlic, minced
- Zest and juice of 1 lemon
- 1/4 cup grated Parmesan cheese
- Salt and freshly ground black pepper, to taste
- Crushed red pepper flakes, for heat (optional)
- Chopped fresh parsley, for garnish

Instructions:

1. Cook the pasta according to the package instructions until al dente. Drain the pasta, reserving 1/2 cup of the pasta cooking water, and set it aside.
2. While the pasta is cooking, heat the olive oil in a large skillet over medium heat. Add the minced garlic and cook for 1-2 minutes, or until fragrant.
3. Add the asparagus pieces to the skillet and sauté for 4-5 minutes, or until they are tender-crisp and bright green.
4. Stir in the lemon zest and lemon juice, then season with salt and freshly ground black pepper to taste. Add crushed red pepper flakes for a bit of heat, if desired.
5. Add the cooked pasta to the skillet with the asparagus and toss everything together until the pasta is evenly coated with the lemon sauce. If the sauce seems too dry, you can add a splash of the reserved pasta cooking water to loosen it up.
6. Stir in the grated Parmesan cheese, then taste and adjust seasoning as needed.
7. Serve the Lemon Asparagus Pasta hot, garnished with chopped fresh parsley.

Enjoy your delicious and vibrant Lemon Asparagus Pasta! It's perfect for a light and refreshing meal, especially during the spring and summer months.

Spaghetti with Meatballs

Ingredients:

For the meatballs:

- 1 pound (about 450g) ground beef
- 1/2 cup breadcrumbs
- 1/4 cup grated Parmesan cheese
- 1/4 cup chopped fresh parsley
- 2 cloves garlic, minced
- 1 egg, beaten
- 1 teaspoon salt
- 1/2 teaspoon black pepper
- Olive oil, for frying

For the spaghetti:

- 8 ounces (about 225g) spaghetti pasta
- 4 cups marinara sauce (homemade or store-bought)
- Grated Parmesan cheese, for serving
- Chopped fresh parsley, for garnish (optional)

Instructions:

1. In a large mixing bowl, combine the ground beef, breadcrumbs, grated Parmesan cheese, chopped fresh parsley, minced garlic, beaten egg, salt, and black pepper. Mix until well combined.
2. Shape the mixture into meatballs, about 1-1.5 inches in diameter. You should get around 20-24 meatballs, depending on the size.
3. Heat a couple of tablespoons of olive oil in a large skillet over medium heat. Add the meatballs to the skillet in a single layer, making sure not to overcrowd the pan. Cook the meatballs for 2-3 minutes on each side, or until they are browned and cooked through. You may need to cook the meatballs in batches.
4. While the meatballs are cooking, bring a large pot of salted water to a boil. Cook the spaghetti according to the package instructions until al dente. Drain the cooked spaghetti and set it aside.
5. In a separate saucepan, heat the marinara sauce over medium heat until heated through.

6. Once the meatballs are cooked and the spaghetti is cooked and drained, assemble the dish. Place a serving of cooked spaghetti on each plate or in a large serving dish. Top with some warm marinara sauce and a few meatballs.
7. Garnish with grated Parmesan cheese and chopped fresh parsley, if desired.
8. Serve the Spaghetti with Meatballs hot, accompanied by extra marinara sauce and Parmesan cheese on the side.

Enjoy your delicious and hearty Spaghetti with Meatballs! It's a timeless favorite that's perfect for a cozy family dinner or any occasion.

Sun-Dried Tomato Pesto Pasta

Ingredients:

For the sun-dried tomato pesto:

- 1 cup sun-dried tomatoes (packed in oil), drained
- 1 cup fresh basil leaves
- 2 cloves garlic
- 1/4 cup pine nuts or walnuts
- 1/2 cup grated Parmesan cheese
- 1/4 cup olive oil
- Salt and freshly ground black pepper, to taste

For the pasta:

- 8 ounces (about 225g) pasta (such as penne, spaghetti, or fettuccine)
- Extra sun-dried tomatoes, chopped, for garnish (optional)
- Grated Parmesan cheese, for serving
- Fresh basil leaves, for garnish (optional)

Instructions:

1. Cook the pasta according to the package instructions until al dente. Drain the pasta, reserving 1/2 cup of the pasta cooking water, and set it aside.
2. While the pasta is cooking, prepare the sun-dried tomato pesto. In a food processor, combine the sun-dried tomatoes, fresh basil leaves, garlic, nuts, and grated Parmesan cheese. Pulse until finely chopped.
3. With the food processor running, gradually add the olive oil in a steady stream until the pesto reaches your desired consistency. You may need to scrape down the sides of the food processor bowl with a spatula.
4. Season the sun-dried tomato pesto with salt and freshly ground black pepper to taste. Adjust the seasoning if necessary.
5. In a large mixing bowl, toss the cooked pasta with the sun-dried tomato pesto until well coated. If the sauce seems too thick, you can add some of the reserved pasta cooking water to thin it out.
6. Serve the sun-dried tomato pesto pasta hot, garnished with extra chopped sun-dried tomatoes, grated Parmesan cheese, and fresh basil leaves, if desired.

Enjoy your delicious and flavorful Sun-Dried Tomato Pesto Pasta! It's perfect for a quick and easy weeknight dinner or a special occasion meal.

Cajun Shrimp Pasta

Ingredients:

- 8 ounces (about 225g) pasta (such as fettuccine, linguine, or penne)
- 1 pound (about 450g) large shrimp, peeled and deveined
- 2 tablespoons Cajun seasoning
- 2 tablespoons olive oil
- 4 cloves garlic, minced
- 1 red bell pepper, thinly sliced
- 1 yellow bell pepper, thinly sliced
- 1 cup cherry tomatoes, halved
- 1 cup chicken broth
- 1 cup heavy cream
- Salt and freshly ground black pepper, to taste
- Chopped fresh parsley, for garnish
- Grated Parmesan cheese, for serving (optional)

Instructions:

1. Cook the pasta according to the package instructions until al dente. Drain the pasta and set it aside.
2. In a large mixing bowl, toss the peeled and deveined shrimp with Cajun seasoning until evenly coated.
3. Heat the olive oil in a large skillet over medium-high heat. Add the seasoned shrimp to the skillet and cook for 2-3 minutes per side, or until they are pink and opaque. Remove the cooked shrimp from the skillet and set them aside.
4. In the same skillet, add the minced garlic and sliced bell peppers. Sauté for 2-3 minutes, or until the peppers are slightly softened.
5. Add the halved cherry tomatoes to the skillet and cook for another 1-2 minutes.
6. Pour the chicken broth into the skillet and bring it to a simmer. Let it cook for 2-3 minutes to reduce slightly.
7. Stir in the heavy cream and bring the mixture to a simmer. Let it cook for another 2-3 minutes, or until the sauce thickens slightly.
8. Return the cooked shrimp to the skillet and toss them with the sauce and vegetables until heated through. Season the sauce with salt and freshly ground black pepper to taste.
9. Add the cooked pasta to the skillet with the Cajun shrimp sauce and toss everything together until the pasta is evenly coated.

10. Serve the Cajun Shrimp Pasta hot, garnished with chopped fresh parsley and grated Parmesan cheese, if desired.

Enjoy your spicy and delicious Cajun Shrimp Pasta! It's perfect for a flavorful dinner that's sure to impress.

Pasta with Sausage and Peppers

Ingredients:

- 8 ounces (about 225g) pasta (such as penne, rigatoni, or spaghetti)
- 1 pound (about 450g) Italian sausage (mild or spicy), casings removed
- 2 tablespoons olive oil
- 1 onion, thinly sliced
- 2 bell peppers (red, green, or yellow), thinly sliced
- 3 cloves garlic, minced
- 1 can (14.5 ounces/400g) diced tomatoes
- 1 teaspoon Italian seasoning
- Salt and freshly ground black pepper, to taste
- Grated Parmesan cheese, for serving (optional)
- Chopped fresh parsley, for garnish (optional)

Instructions:

1. Cook the pasta according to the package instructions until al dente. Drain the pasta and set it aside.
2. While the pasta is cooking, heat the olive oil in a large skillet over medium-high heat. Add the Italian sausage to the skillet and cook, breaking it apart with a wooden spoon, until browned and cooked through, about 5-7 minutes. Remove the cooked sausage from the skillet and set it aside.
3. In the same skillet, add the sliced onions and bell peppers. Sauté for 4-5 minutes, or until the vegetables are softened.
4. Add the minced garlic to the skillet and cook for an additional 1-2 minutes, until fragrant.
5. Stir in the diced tomatoes (with their juices) and Italian seasoning. Bring the mixture to a simmer and let it cook for 5-7 minutes, or until the sauce has thickened slightly.
6. Return the cooked sausage to the skillet and toss it with the peppers and onions until heated through. Season the sauce with salt and freshly ground black pepper to taste.
7. Add the cooked pasta to the skillet with the sausage and peppers and toss everything together until the pasta is evenly coated with the sauce.
8. Serve the Pasta with Sausage and Peppers hot, garnished with grated Parmesan cheese and chopped fresh parsley, if desired.

Enjoy your delicious and satisfying Pasta with Sausage and Peppers! It's perfect for a hearty weeknight dinner or a casual gathering with family and friends.

Baked Manicotti

Ingredients:

- 1 box (8 ounces/225g) manicotti pasta shells
- 2 cups ricotta cheese
- 1 cup shredded mozzarella cheese
- 1/2 cup grated Parmesan cheese
- 1 egg, lightly beaten
- 2 tablespoons chopped fresh parsley
- 1 teaspoon dried oregano
- 1/2 teaspoon garlic powder
- Salt and freshly ground black pepper, to taste
- 2 cups marinara sauce (homemade or store-bought)
- Additional shredded mozzarella cheese, for topping
- Additional grated Parmesan cheese, for topping
- Chopped fresh basil, for garnish (optional)

Instructions:

1. Preheat your oven to 375°F (190°C). Grease a 9x13-inch baking dish with cooking spray or butter.
2. Cook the manicotti pasta shells according to the package instructions until they are slightly undercooked, about 7-8 minutes. Drain the pasta and rinse it under cold water to stop the cooking process. Set the cooked pasta shells aside.
3. In a mixing bowl, combine the ricotta cheese, shredded mozzarella cheese, grated Parmesan cheese, beaten egg, chopped fresh parsley, dried oregano, garlic powder, salt, and black pepper. Mix until well combined.
4. Spoon the cheese mixture into a large zip-top bag or piping bag fitted with a large round tip. Alternatively, you can use a spoon to fill the manicotti shells.
5. Spread a thin layer of marinara sauce on the bottom of the prepared baking dish.
6. Carefully fill each manicotti shell with the cheese mixture and arrange them in a single layer in the baking dish.
7. Pour the remaining marinara sauce over the filled manicotti shells, covering them evenly.
8. Sprinkle additional shredded mozzarella cheese and grated Parmesan cheese over the top of the sauce.
9. Cover the baking dish with aluminum foil and bake in the preheated oven for 25-30 minutes, or until the cheese is melted and bubbly.

10. Remove the foil and continue baking for an additional 5-10 minutes, or until the cheese is golden brown and bubbly.
11. Remove the baked manicotti from the oven and let it cool for a few minutes before serving.
12. Garnish with chopped fresh basil, if desired, and serve hot.

Enjoy your delicious Baked Manicotti! It's perfect for a cozy family dinner or a special occasion meal.

Mediterranean Orzo Salad

Ingredients:

For the salad:

- 1 cup orzo pasta
- 1 cucumber, diced
- 1 cup cherry tomatoes, halved
- 1/2 cup Kalamata olives, pitted and halved
- 1/4 cup red onion, thinly sliced
- 1/4 cup crumbled feta cheese
- 2 tablespoons chopped fresh parsley
- 2 tablespoons chopped fresh mint (optional)

For the lemon vinaigrette:

- 1/4 cup extra virgin olive oil
- 2 tablespoons fresh lemon juice
- 1 teaspoon Dijon mustard
- 1 clove garlic, minced
- 1/2 teaspoon dried oregano
- Salt and freshly ground black pepper, to taste

Instructions:

1. Cook the orzo pasta according to the package instructions until al dente. Drain the pasta and rinse it under cold water to stop the cooking process. Transfer the cooked orzo to a large mixing bowl and let it cool slightly.
2. While the orzo is cooking, prepare the vegetables. Dice the cucumber, halve the cherry tomatoes, pit and halve the Kalamata olives, and thinly slice the red onion. Chop the fresh parsley and mint, if using.
3. In a small mixing bowl, whisk together the ingredients for the lemon vinaigrette: olive oil, lemon juice, Dijon mustard, minced garlic, dried oregano, salt, and black pepper.
4. Add the diced cucumber, halved cherry tomatoes, Kalamata olives, sliced red onion, crumbled feta cheese, chopped parsley, and chopped mint (if using) to the bowl with the cooked orzo.
5. Pour the lemon vinaigrette over the salad ingredients in the bowl. Toss everything together until well combined and evenly coated with the dressing.
6. Taste and adjust seasoning, adding more salt, pepper, or lemon juice if desired.

7. Cover the bowl with plastic wrap and refrigerate the Mediterranean Orzo Salad for at least 30 minutes to allow the flavors to meld together.
8. Before serving, give the salad a final toss to redistribute the dressing. Garnish with additional chopped parsley or mint, if desired.
9. Serve the Mediterranean Orzo Salad chilled or at room temperature as a refreshing side dish or light main course.

Enjoy your delicious and vibrant Mediterranean Orzo Salad! It's perfect for picnics, potlucks, or any summer gathering.

Tuna Casserole

Ingredients:

- 8 ounces (about 225g) pasta (such as egg noodles or rotini)
- 2 cans (5 ounces/142g each) tuna, drained and flaked
- 1 cup frozen peas, thawed
- 1 cup sliced mushrooms (optional)
- 1/4 cup chopped onion
- 2 cloves garlic, minced
- 2 tablespoons butter
- 2 tablespoons all-purpose flour
- 1 1/2 cups milk
- 1 cup shredded cheddar cheese
- 1/2 cup breadcrumbs
- Salt and freshly ground black pepper, to taste
- Chopped fresh parsley, for garnish (optional)

Instructions:

1. Preheat your oven to 375°F (190°C). Grease a 9x13-inch baking dish with butter or cooking spray.
2. Cook the pasta according to the package instructions until al dente. Drain the pasta and set it aside.
3. In a large skillet, melt the butter over medium heat. Add the chopped onion and minced garlic, and cook for 2-3 minutes until softened and fragrant.
4. If using, add the sliced mushrooms to the skillet and cook for an additional 3-4 minutes until they release their moisture and start to brown.
5. Sprinkle the flour over the vegetables in the skillet and stir to combine. Cook for 1-2 minutes to cook off the raw flour taste.
6. Gradually pour in the milk while whisking constantly to prevent lumps from forming. Cook the sauce, stirring frequently, until it thickens, about 5-7 minutes.
7. Stir in the shredded cheddar cheese until melted and smooth. Season the sauce with salt and freshly ground black pepper to taste.
8. In a large mixing bowl, combine the cooked pasta, flaked tuna, thawed peas, and cheese sauce. Mix until everything is evenly coated.
9. Transfer the tuna and pasta mixture to the prepared baking dish and spread it out into an even layer.
10. In a small bowl, combine the breadcrumbs with a tablespoon of melted butter. Sprinkle the breadcrumb mixture evenly over the top of the casserole.

11. Bake the tuna casserole in the preheated oven for 25-30 minutes, or until the breadcrumbs are golden brown and the casserole is bubbly.
12. Remove the casserole from the oven and let it cool for a few minutes before serving.
13. Garnish the tuna casserole with chopped fresh parsley, if desired, and serve hot.

Enjoy your delicious and comforting Tuna Casserole! It's perfect for a cozy weeknight dinner or potluck gathering.

Pasta with Roasted Garlic and Cherry Tomatoes

Ingredients:

- 8 ounces (about 225g) pasta (such as spaghetti, linguine, or penne)
- 2 cups cherry tomatoes, halved
- 6 cloves garlic, peeled
- 1/4 cup extra virgin olive oil
- Salt and freshly ground black pepper, to taste
- Red pepper flakes, for heat (optional)
- Grated Parmesan cheese, for serving
- Chopped fresh basil or parsley, for garnish (optional)

Instructions:

1. Preheat your oven to 400°F (200°C).
2. Place the halved cherry tomatoes and peeled garlic cloves on a baking sheet. Drizzle them with olive oil and season with salt and freshly ground black pepper to taste. Toss everything together until the tomatoes and garlic are evenly coated with oil and seasoning.
3. Roast the cherry tomatoes and garlic in the preheated oven for 20-25 minutes, or until the tomatoes are softened and starting to caramelize, and the garlic is golden brown and fragrant. Keep an eye on them to prevent burning.
4. While the tomatoes and garlic are roasting, cook the pasta according to the package instructions until al dente. Drain the pasta, reserving 1/2 cup of the pasta cooking water, and set it aside.
5. Once the cherry tomatoes and garlic are roasted, remove them from the oven and let them cool slightly. Mash the roasted garlic cloves with a fork to create a paste.
6. In a large mixing bowl, combine the cooked pasta with the roasted cherry tomatoes, mashed garlic paste, and any juices from the baking sheet. Toss everything together until the pasta is evenly coated with the tomato and garlic mixture. If the sauce seems too thick, you can add some of the reserved pasta cooking water to thin it out.
7. Season the pasta with additional salt, freshly ground black pepper, and red pepper flakes for heat, if desired.
8. Serve the Pasta with Roasted Garlic and Cherry Tomatoes hot, garnished with grated Parmesan cheese and chopped fresh basil or parsley, if desired.

Enjoy your delicious and flavorful Pasta with Roasted Garlic and Cherry Tomatoes! It's perfect for a quick and easy weeknight dinner or a light and refreshing summer meal.

Pumpkin Ravioli with Brown Butter Sage Sauce

Ingredients:

For the pumpkin ravioli:

- 1 package (about 24 ounces/680g) fresh or frozen pumpkin ravioli
- 1 cup canned pumpkin puree
- 1/2 cup grated Parmesan cheese
- 1/4 teaspoon ground nutmeg
- Salt and freshly ground black pepper, to taste

For the brown butter sage sauce:

- 1/2 cup (1 stick) unsalted butter
- 8-10 fresh sage leaves
- 1/4 cup grated Parmesan cheese, for serving
- Toasted pine nuts, for garnish (optional)

Instructions:

1. Cook the pumpkin ravioli according to the package instructions until they are al dente. Drain the ravioli and set them aside.
2. In a mixing bowl, combine the canned pumpkin puree, grated Parmesan cheese, ground nutmeg, salt, and freshly ground black pepper. Mix until well combined.
3. Place a spoonful of the pumpkin mixture onto each ravioli wrapper. Brush the edges of the wrappers with water, then place another wrapper on top of each filled one. Press down firmly around the edges to seal the ravioli, ensuring there are no air pockets.
4. Bring a large pot of salted water to a boil. Carefully add the pumpkin ravioli to the boiling water and cook according to the package instructions, usually 3-4 minutes for fresh ravioli or 5-6 minutes for frozen ravioli. Drain the cooked ravioli and set them aside.
5. While the ravioli are cooking, prepare the brown butter sage sauce. In a large skillet, melt the unsalted butter over medium heat. Add the fresh sage leaves to the skillet and cook them for 1-2 minutes, or until they are crispy and fragrant. Be careful not to burn the butter.
6. Once the butter is golden brown and nutty in aroma, remove the skillet from the heat.
7. Add the cooked pumpkin ravioli to the skillet with the brown butter sage sauce. Gently toss to coat the ravioli evenly with the sauce.

8. Serve the Pumpkin Ravioli with Brown Butter Sage Sauce hot, garnished with grated Parmesan cheese and toasted pine nuts, if desired.

Enjoy your delicious and indulgent Pumpkin Ravioli with Brown Butter Sage Sauce! It's perfect for a special occasion or any time you want to treat yourself to a gourmet meal.

Chicken and Spinach Alfredo Lasagna

Ingredients:

- 9 lasagna noodles
- 2 cups cooked and shredded chicken breast
- 2 cups fresh spinach leaves
- 2 cups Alfredo sauce (homemade or store-bought)
- 1 cup shredded mozzarella cheese
- 1/2 cup grated Parmesan cheese
- Salt and freshly ground black pepper, to taste
- 1 tablespoon olive oil
- 2 cloves garlic, minced
- 1/2 teaspoon dried Italian herbs (such as oregano, basil, and thyme)
- Chopped fresh parsley, for garnish (optional)

Instructions:

1. Preheat your oven to 375°F (190°C). Grease a 9x13-inch baking dish with cooking spray or butter.
2. Cook the lasagna noodles according to the package instructions until al dente. Drain the noodles and rinse them under cold water to prevent sticking. Set the noodles aside.
3. In a large skillet, heat the olive oil over medium heat. Add the minced garlic and cook for 1-2 minutes until fragrant.
4. Add the fresh spinach leaves to the skillet and cook, stirring occasionally, until wilted, about 2-3 minutes. Season the spinach with salt, freshly ground black pepper, and dried Italian herbs. Remove the skillet from the heat and set it aside.
5. In a mixing bowl, combine the cooked and shredded chicken breast with 1 cup of Alfredo sauce. Mix until the chicken is evenly coated with the sauce.
6. Spread a thin layer of Alfredo sauce on the bottom of the prepared baking dish. Arrange 3 lasagna noodles over the sauce, slightly overlapping them if necessary.
7. Spread half of the chicken Alfredo mixture over the noodles, followed by half of the cooked spinach. Sprinkle with half of the shredded mozzarella cheese and grated Parmesan cheese.
8. Repeat the layers with the remaining lasagna noodles, chicken Alfredo mixture, spinach, and cheeses.
9. Cover the baking dish with aluminum foil and bake the lasagna in the preheated oven for 25-30 minutes.

10. Remove the foil and bake the lasagna for an additional 10-15 minutes, or until the cheese is melted and bubbly and the edges are golden brown.
11. Remove the lasagna from the oven and let it cool for a few minutes before slicing.
12. Garnish the Chicken and Spinach Alfredo Lasagna with chopped fresh parsley, if desired, and serve hot.

Enjoy your delicious and creamy Chicken and Spinach Alfredo Lasagna! It's perfect for a cozy family dinner or a special occasion meal.

Penne alla Norma

Ingredients:

- 12 ounces (about 340g) penne pasta
- 1 large eggplant, diced
- 4 tablespoons olive oil, divided
- 4 cloves garlic, minced
- 1 can (14.5 ounces/411g) diced tomatoes
- 1/2 teaspoon red pepper flakes (optional)
- Salt and freshly ground black pepper, to taste
- 1/4 cup chopped fresh basil leaves, plus more for garnish
- 1/2 cup grated ricotta salata cheese, plus more for garnish

Instructions:

1. Cook the penne pasta according to the package instructions until al dente. Drain the pasta and set it aside.
2. While the pasta is cooking, heat 2 tablespoons of olive oil in a large skillet over medium heat. Add the diced eggplant to the skillet and cook, stirring occasionally, until the eggplant is golden brown and softened, about 10-12 minutes. Remove the cooked eggplant from the skillet and set it aside.
3. In the same skillet, add the remaining 2 tablespoons of olive oil. Add the minced garlic and red pepper flakes (if using) to the skillet and cook for 1-2 minutes, or until the garlic is fragrant.
4. Add the diced tomatoes to the skillet, along with their juices. Cook the tomatoes, stirring occasionally, for 5-7 minutes, or until they start to break down and thicken slightly.
5. Return the cooked eggplant to the skillet with the tomatoes. Season the sauce with salt and freshly ground black pepper to taste. Stir in the chopped fresh basil leaves.
6. Add the cooked penne pasta to the skillet with the sauce and toss everything together until the pasta is evenly coated.
7. Remove the skillet from the heat and sprinkle the grated ricotta salata cheese over the top of the pasta. Toss gently to combine.
8. Serve the Penne alla Norma hot, garnished with additional chopped fresh basil leaves and grated ricotta salata cheese.

Enjoy your delicious and flavorful Penne alla Norma! It's a perfect dish for showcasing the flavors of Sicilian cuisine.

Pasta with Artichokes and Sun-Dried Tomatoes

Ingredients:

- 8 ounces (about 225g) pasta (such as penne, fusilli, or spaghetti)
- 1 can (14 ounces/400g) artichoke hearts, drained and quartered
- 1/2 cup sun-dried tomatoes, drained and chopped
- 2 cloves garlic, minced
- 2 tablespoons olive oil
- 1/4 cup grated Parmesan cheese, plus more for serving
- 2 tablespoons chopped fresh basil or parsley
- Salt and freshly ground black pepper, to taste
- Crushed red pepper flakes, for heat (optional)

Instructions:

1. Cook the pasta according to the package instructions until al dente. Drain the pasta, reserving 1/2 cup of the pasta cooking water, and set it aside.
2. While the pasta is cooking, heat the olive oil in a large skillet over medium heat. Add the minced garlic to the skillet and cook for 1-2 minutes, or until fragrant.
3. Add the artichoke hearts and sun-dried tomatoes to the skillet. Cook, stirring occasionally, for 3-4 minutes, or until the artichokes are heated through and the sun-dried tomatoes are softened.
4. Season the artichokes and sun-dried tomatoes with salt, freshly ground black pepper, and crushed red pepper flakes (if using), to taste.
5. Add the cooked pasta to the skillet with the artichokes and sun-dried tomatoes. Toss everything together until the pasta is evenly coated with the mixture.
6. If the sauce seems too dry, you can add some of the reserved pasta cooking water to loosen it up.
7. Stir in the grated Parmesan cheese and chopped fresh basil or parsley. Toss gently to combine.
8. Serve the Pasta with Artichokes and Sun-Dried Tomatoes hot, garnished with additional grated Parmesan cheese, if desired.

Enjoy your delicious and flavorful Pasta with Artichokes and Sun-Dried Tomatoes! It's perfect for a quick and easy weeknight dinner or a special occasion meal.

Beef and Mushroom Stroganoff

Ingredients:

- 1 pound (about 450g) beef sirloin steak, thinly sliced
- 8 ounces (about 225g) mushrooms, sliced
- 1 onion, finely chopped
- 2 cloves garlic, minced
- 2 tablespoons butter
- 2 tablespoons all-purpose flour
- 1 cup beef broth
- 1 cup sour cream
- 2 teaspoons Dijon mustard
- 1 teaspoon Worcestershire sauce
- Salt and freshly ground black pepper, to taste
- Chopped fresh parsley, for garnish (optional)
- Cooked egg noodles or rice, for serving

Instructions:

1. In a large skillet, melt the butter over medium-high heat. Add the thinly sliced beef sirloin to the skillet and cook, stirring occasionally, until browned on all sides. Remove the beef from the skillet and set it aside.
2. In the same skillet, add the sliced mushrooms and chopped onion. Cook, stirring occasionally, until the mushrooms are golden brown and the onions are softened, about 5-7 minutes.
3. Add the minced garlic to the skillet and cook for an additional 1-2 minutes, until fragrant.
4. Sprinkle the flour over the mushrooms and onions in the skillet. Stir to combine and cook for 1-2 minutes to cook off the raw flour taste.
5. Gradually pour in the beef broth while stirring constantly, scraping up any browned bits from the bottom of the skillet.
6. Bring the mixture to a simmer and cook for 2-3 minutes, or until the sauce thickens slightly.
7. Stir in the sour cream, Dijon mustard, and Worcestershire sauce until smooth and well combined. Season the sauce with salt and freshly ground black pepper to taste.
8. Return the cooked beef slices to the skillet with the mushroom sauce. Cook, stirring occasionally, until the beef is heated through, about 2-3 minutes.

9. Serve the Beef and Mushroom Stroganoff hot, garnished with chopped fresh parsley, if desired. Serve over cooked egg noodles or rice.

Enjoy your delicious and comforting Beef and Mushroom Stroganoff! It's perfect for a cozy family dinner or a special occasion meal.

Creamy Bacon CarbonaraSpicy Arrabbiata Pasta

Ingredients:

- 8 ounces (about 225g) spaghetti or fettuccine
- 6 slices bacon, chopped
- 3 cloves garlic, minced
- 2 large eggs
- 1/2 cup grated Parmesan cheese
- 1/4 cup heavy cream
- Salt and freshly ground black pepper, to taste
- Chopped fresh parsley, for garnish (optional)

Instructions:

1. Cook the pasta according to the package instructions until al dente. Drain the pasta, reserving 1/2 cup of the pasta cooking water, and set it aside.
2. In a large skillet, cook the chopped bacon over medium heat until crispy. Remove the cooked bacon from the skillet and set it aside, leaving the bacon drippings in the skillet.
3. Add the minced garlic to the skillet with the bacon drippings and cook for 1-2 minutes, until fragrant.
4. In a mixing bowl, whisk together the eggs, grated Parmesan cheese, and heavy cream until well combined.
5. Add the cooked pasta to the skillet with the garlic and bacon drippings. Toss to coat the pasta evenly.
6. Remove the skillet from the heat and quickly pour the egg and cheese mixture over the pasta. Toss the pasta continuously until the sauce thickens and coats the pasta, about 1-2 minutes. If the sauce is too thick, you can add some of the reserved pasta cooking water to thin it out.
7. Stir in the cooked bacon and season the pasta with salt and freshly ground black pepper to taste.
8. Serve the Creamy Bacon Carbonara hot, garnished with chopped fresh parsley, if desired.

Spicy Arrabbiata Pasta:

Ingredients:

- 8 ounces (about 225g) penne or spaghetti
- 2 tablespoons olive oil
- 3 cloves garlic, minced
- 1/2 teaspoon red pepper flakes (adjust to taste for desired spiciness)
- 1 can (14.5 ounces/411g) diced tomatoes
- Salt and freshly ground black pepper, to taste
- Chopped fresh basil, for garnish (optional)
- Grated Parmesan cheese, for serving

Instructions:

1. Cook the pasta according to the package instructions until al dente. Drain the pasta and set it aside.
2. In a large skillet, heat the olive oil over medium heat. Add the minced garlic and red pepper flakes to the skillet and cook for 1-2 minutes, until fragrant.
3. Add the diced tomatoes to the skillet, along with their juices. Bring the mixture to a simmer and cook for 10-12 minutes, stirring occasionally, until the sauce thickens slightly.
4. Season the sauce with salt and freshly ground black pepper to taste.
5. Add the cooked pasta to the skillet with the spicy tomato sauce. Toss to coat the pasta evenly with the sauce.
6. Serve the Spicy Arrabbiata Pasta hot, garnished with chopped fresh basil and grated Parmesan cheese.

Enjoy your delicious and flavorful Creamy Bacon Carbonara and Spicy Arrabbiata Pasta! They're perfect for a satisfying and comforting meal.

www.ingramcontent.com/pod-product-compliance
Lightning Source LLC
LaVergne TN
LVHW061947070526
838199LV00060B/4011